ALASKA GEOGRAPHIC®

VOLUME 16, NUMBER 4

THE COPPER TRAIL

The Alaska Geographic Society

To teach many more to better know and use our natural resources

Editor: Penny Rennick
Associate Editor: Kathy Doogan
General Manager: Phyllis Marchese
Production Coordinator: Lynne Hanson
Cartographics: Steven Fisher

Board of Directors:
Robert A. Henning, *President,*
Judge Thomas Stewart, Phyllis Henning,
Jim Brooks, Charles Herbert, Celia Hunter,
Byron Mallott, Dr. Glen Olds, Penny Rennick
National Advisors:
Gilbert Grosvenor, Bradford Washburn,
Dr. John Reed

ALASKA GEOGRAPHIC®, ISSN 0361-1353, is published quarterly by The Alaska Geographic Society, 137 East 7th, Anchorage, Alaska 99501. Second-class postage paid in Anchorage, Alaska 99509-3370 and additional offices. Printed in U.S.A. Copyright © 1989 by The Alaska Geographic Society. All rights reserved. Registered trademark: Alaska Geographic, ISSN 0361-1353; Key title Alaska Geographic.

THE ALASKA GEOGRAPHIC SOCIETY is a non-profit organization exploring new frontiers of knowledge across the lands of the Polar Rim, putting the geography book back in the classroom, exploring new methods of teaching and learning—sharing in the excitment of discovery in man's wonderful new world north of 51°16'.

MEMBERS OF THE SOCIETY receive *ALASKA GEOGRAPHIC®*, a quality magazine that devotes each quarterly issue to monographic in-depth coverage of a northern geographic region or resource-oriented subject.

MEMBERSHIP DUES in The Alaska Geographic Society are $39 per year, $43 to non-U.S. addresses. ($31.20 of the $39 yearly dues is for a one-year subscription to *ALASKA GEOGRAPHIC®*.) Order from The Alaska Geographic Society, P.O. Box 93370, Anchorage, Alaska 99509-3370; phone (907) 258-2515.

PRICE TO NONMEMBERS THIS ISSUE, $17.95 ($21.95 Canadian)

MATERIALS SOUGHT: The editors of *ALASKA GEOGRAPHIC®* seek a wide variety of informative material on the lands north of 51°16' on geographic subjects—anything to do with resources and their uses (with heavy emphasis on quality color photography)—from all the lands of the Polar Rim and the economically related North Pacific Rim. We cannot be responsible for submissions not accompanied by sufficient postage for return by certified mail. Payments are made for all material upon publication.

CHANGE OF ADDRESS: The post office does not automatically forward *ALASKA GEOGRAPHIC®* when you move. To ensure continuous service, notify us six weeks before moving. Send us your new address and zip code, and if possible send a mailing label from a copy of *ALASKA GEOGRAPHIC®*. Send this information to *ALASKA GEOGRAPHIC®*, P.O. Box 93370, Anchorage, Alaska 99509-3370.

MAILING LISTS: We have begun making our members' names and addresses available to carefully screened publications and companies whose products and activities may be of interest to you. If you would prefer not to receive such mailings, please advise us, and include your mailing label (or your name and address if label is not available).

ABOUT THIS ISSUE: Steven W. Nelson of the U.S. Geological Survey writes about the geological and geographical features of the Copper River country for this issue. His work complements the historical review by Nicki Nielsen, author of two books on the Cordova area. Nicki also contributes closer looks at three of the Copper Trail's most famous pioneers, Michael J. Heney, Eustace P. Ziegler and Richard Davis. Fisherman and writer Dan Strickland gives readers a firsthand look at the life of a Copper River fisherman. We thank Mike O'Neill, member of a pioneer Cordova and McCarthy family, for information about his uncle, John B. O'Neill; and Steve McCutcheon, a native son of the Copper River country, for a glimpse of early day Chitina.

As always, we are grateful to the many photographers whose images capture the spirit of the Copper Trail.

Editor's note: Mountain elevations for this issue are from the *Dictionary of Alaska Place Names* (1967), by Donald J. Orth. Populations are from the Alaska Department of Commerce and Economic Development. Spelling of "Kennecott" varies, but generally the town and mining company are spelled with an "e"; the river and glacier with an "i". The *Dictionary of Alaska Place Names* explains: The mining company took its name from Kennicott Glacier, but misspelled Kennicott, dropping the "i" and adding the second "e". The post office, which operated from 1908 to 1938, adopted the spelling used by the company, and the town became Kennecott. However, in recent years the spelling has reverted in many cases to Kennicott, after Robert Kennicott, leader of the Western Union Telegraph Expedition until his death at Nulato in 1866.

The Library of Congress has cataloged this serial publication as follows:

Alaska Geographic. v.1-
[Anchorage, Alaska Geographic Society] 1972-
v. ill. (part col.). 23 x 31 cm.
Quarterly
Official publication of The Alaska Geographic Society.
Key title; Alaska geographic, ISSN 0361-1353.

1. Alaska—Description and travel—1959-
—Periodicals. I. Alaska Geographic Society.

F901.A266 917.98'04'505 72-92087

Library of Congress 75[79112] MARC-S

Postmaster: Send address changes to
ALASKA GEOGRAPHIC®
P.O. Box 93370
Anchorage, Alaska 99509-3370

PREVIOUS PAGE—*A gillnetter glides past the Cordova city dock, while the Heney Range rises in the background.* (Steve Moffitt)

COVER—*Remains of the Kennecott Copper Co.'s mill tower above the former company town that boomed in early decades of the 20th century.* (Third Eye Photography)

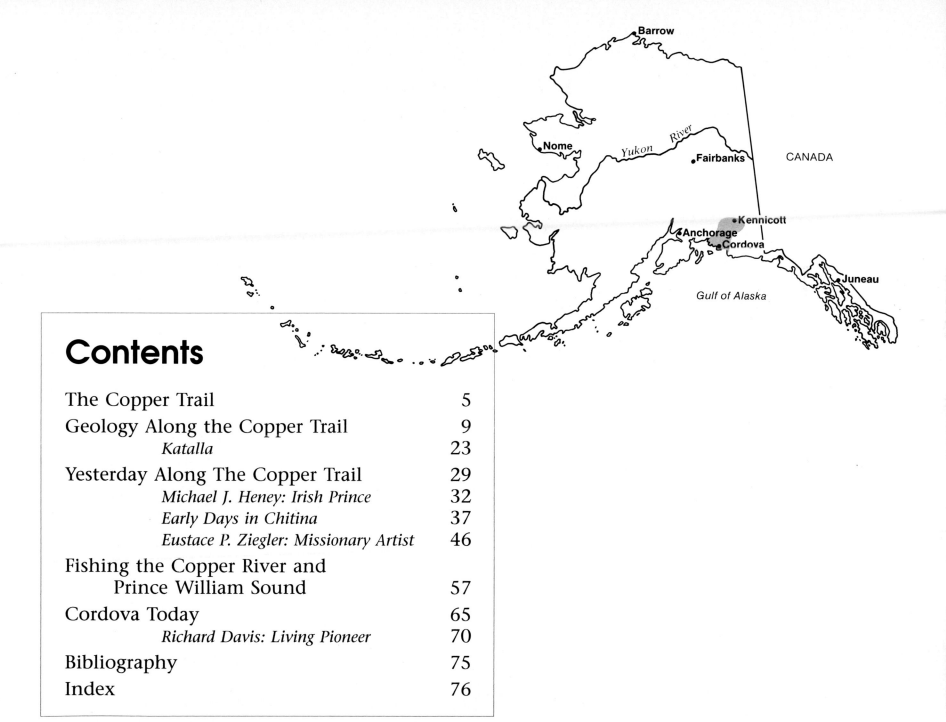

Barrow

Nome

Yukon River

Fairbanks

CANADA

Kennicott

Anchorage
Cordova

Juneau

Gulf of Alaska

Contents

The Copper Trail

The Copper Trail begins on the steep slopes of the Wrangell Mountains, beneath the snowy summit of Mount Blackburn. Here, within the boundaries of Wrangell-Saint Elias National Park, geological forces combined fortuitously to produce some of the richest copper deposits ever found. For more than a millenium prior to the arrival of white men, Ahtna and coastal Eyak Athabascans had traded items made with this malleable metal to other native groups along the coast and in Alaska's Interior. This trade spread word of the copper's existence, capturing the attention of European and Russian explorers.

Western adventurers tried several times unsuccessfully to ascend the river the Athabascans knew as *Atna*, and the white men called *Copper*. But narrow canyons, ferocious currents and inhospitable weather joined with a rugged mountain barrier to block the inadequate attempts of mortal man. Not until Lt. Henry Allen's epic journey up the Copper River in 1885 were Westerners able to concentrate their search for the source of the copper. With the aid of an Indian leader, Nicolai, Allen explored the Chitina River valley. Thirteen years later, U.S. Geological Survey geologists Oscar Rohn and F.C. Schrader outlined the geology of the region, and in 1900 the copper bonanza was pinpointed on a ridge

The Copper River, only river to breach the Chugach Mountains, begins on the north side of the Wrangells, skirts the mountains on the west, flows southward across an upland, cuts through the Chugach Mountains and spreads out in a magnificent delta east of Cordova on the Gulf of Alaska coast. (Steve McCutcheon)

just north of McCarthy and overlooking Kennicott Glacier.

Efforts to mine the copper and ship the ore to a smelter generated the next stage of the Copper Trail, one of high finance and heroic effort in the building of the Copper River & Northwestern Railway. In the end, the trail forged with copper also produced a city, Cordova, and it is this community that remains the major legacy of the Copper Trail.

This issue focuses on the lower reaches of Copper River country: Cordova and the Copper River delta — largest undeveloped delta on the western coast of North America — and the

Once the "fun" town for employees at Kennecott, McCarthy is now a sleepy settlement near the confluence of McCarthy Creek and Kennicott River. Backcountry recreation in Wrangell-Saint Elias National Park has stirred the community a bit, but the handful of residents remain isolated at the end of the 61-mile Edgerton Highway. (Steve McCutcheon)

portion of southeastern Prince William Sound most closely tied to Cordova. For an in-depth look at the country beyond the coastal mountains, see *Wrangell-Saint Elias, International Mountain Wilderness,* Vol. 8, No. 1, of the *ALASKA GEOGRAPHIC®* series.

ABOVE: *Memories of McCarthy hang on the wall of McCarthy Lodge. John B. O'Neill, whose father had come to the country to work on the railroad, operated a store in McCarthy and had an interest in several mining properties in the region. When the mine and railroad ceased operating, O'Neill closed his store and moved to Anchorage where, with his brother Harry, he bought the Richmond Bar and Cafe (at the current location of the Gaslight).* (Harry Walker)

RIGHT: *The tiny community of Chitina lies along the Edgerton Highway just before it reaches the Copper River. Motorists make a sharp turn toward the river, squeeze through a narrow gap in the ridge, descend a steep embankment on a narrow road and come out on the bridge across the Copper River (visible at left center). The road to McCarthy continues at left. Just to the south, the waters of the Copper are joined by those of the Chitina. In this photo, the Copper comes in from the left.* (Charles E. Kay)

Geology Along The Copper Trail

By Steven W. Nelson

Editor's note: *Steve Nelson has studied extensively the geological framework of Prince William Sound and the lower Copper River country as a geologist for the U. S. Geological Survey in Anchorage.*

Geologic Terranes

Geologists have identified four geologic terranes in the general area of the Copper Trail. Each terrane is composed of rocks vastly different from rocks in adjacent terranes, and each is separated from the others by faults. Geologic

Following a prolonged freezing spell, brush and trees along the Copper River Highway are free of most frost and snow. The Chugach Mountains at mile 25 form the backdrop. (Ruth Fairall)

evidence, especially the geographic distribution of fossils (paleogeography), the wander of the magnetic pole (paleomagnetism) and large movements of the earth's crust (plate tectonics), indicates that these terranes may have come from places far removed from their present position in Alaska. Some may actually have originated in the tropics.

From north to south the terranes are called Wrangellia, Chugach, Prince William and Yakutat. Together these terranes form a portion of the Alaska part of the North American plate, one of 10 major plates that make up the earth's crust. (See Figure 1.) The Chugach, Prince William and Yakutat terranes, which include large areas under water, are bounded on their southern margins by seismically active faults. The Pacific Ocean floor (Pacific plate) is traveling under (subducting)

more than 3,800 square miles and that overlies older rocks of the Wrangellia terrane. This volcanic sequence may represent the extreme eastern end of the Aleutian system of volcanoes that have formed in response to the subduction and subsequent melting of the Pacific plate under the North American plate. The volcanic rocks range in age from Miocene to Holocene (1 billion to 20 million years old) and are well-exposed in several volcanoes, some of which are more than 16,000 feet high.

The Copper River Basin, adjacent to the Wrangell Mountains, probably developed in response to forces associated with subduction along the Alaska continental margin. Throughout the past few million years the basin has been periodically filled with, and free of, glacial ice. In ice-free periods, when glaciers were confined to higher alpine areas where they blocked valleys leading out of the basin, a large lake — glacial Lake Atna — intermittently filled the basin. During and following the last major glaciation, Lake Atna covered more than 2,000 square miles; final drainage of the lake occurred about 10,000 years ago. Thick, extensive lake, stream and glacial deposits that accumulated on the lake floor are now well-exposed in the prominent bluffs that line the Copper River.

The Copper River is the main drainage of the Copper River Basin, and the river's course is somewhat anomalous as it cuts through the rugged Chugach Mountains. It is possible that the river's channel was established prior to the uplift of the mountains, and that the rate of erosion kept pace with uplift and formation of the mountains. Subsequent glaciations probably contributed to the maintenance of the river's path.

Chugach Terrane

The Chugach terrane includes the Chugach Mountains, which rise from sea level to more than 13,000 feet, and many glaciers, some of which terminate in the sea. The typical rocks of this terrane consist of Mesozoic (66 to 200 million years old) deep-sea sedimentary and oceanic volcanic rocks that form a continuous belt approximately 1,200 miles long and 35 to 60 miles wide. This band borders the Gulf of Alaska and embraces the Saint Elias and Kenai mountains. Composition of the sedimentary rocks indicates extensive erosion of an old volcanic arc and subsequent deposition by turbidity currents

TOP: *Erosion from the Chugach Mountains has built up a fringe of coastal lowlands, much of which is forested. This typical forest edge consists of scraggly western hemlock and an understory of alder, bunchberry, mosses and in the mid-foreground a* **Vaccinium** *(heath family).* (Ruth Fairall)

RIGHT: *A thick blanket of snow insulates Heiden Canyon and the Chugach Mountains west of the Copper River.* (Steve McCutcheon)

in the ocean. Concurrent with the sedimentation cycles, large areas of submarine volcanism produced lavas that were later mixed with the turbidity deposits by plate movements that brought the Chugach terrane from its original position of about the latitude of California to its present resting site in Alaska. The southern boundary of the Chugach terrane is the Contact fault system.

The Chugach terrane contains many gold mines and a few major copper mines that were active in the early 1900s. These discoveries were made by prospectors as they prepared for travel to the Klondike gold fields to the north.

Prince William Terrane

The geography of the Prince William terrane is typified by the fiordlike pattern of the Prince William Sound coastline and parts of Kodiak Island. This terrane forms a belt more than 60 miles wide that extends from just east of the Copper River and Prince William Sound areas southwestward beneath the continental shelf and continental slope off the Kodiak archipelago, a distance of about 550 miles. The rocks comprising the Prince William terrane are deep-sea-fan turbidities (sedimentary rocks deposited by turbidity currents and composed of alternating layers of sandstone, siltstone and slate) and associated marine volcanic rocks similar to those of the Chugach terrane, but younger in age. The Chugach and Prince William terranes were added to Alaska about 50 million years ago during a collision that resulted in the rocks being folded and faulted. Later glaciation has produced the ice-carved fiords of Prince William Sound.

The actual point of origin for the rocks of the Prince William terrane is still debated. Fossil evidence suggests that the rocks formed at a latitude near their present position, whereas paleomagnetic data suggests as much as 2,500 miles of northward movement. Some lithified gravel deposits found in the Prince William terrane contain pebbles and boulders of a distinctive type of volcanic rock that is found only in northern Mexico and nowhere else along western North America, also suggesting a distant point of origin.

Submarine volcanism that formed the large piles of volcanic rocks like those seen at Ellamar, about 40 miles northwest of Cordova, and at Knight Island in western Prince William Sound produced many copper deposits that were mined in the early 1900s. This marine volcanism concentrated along small segments of ocean rifts similar to those found off the coast of Washington and British Columbia. The characteristic feature of rocks formed this way is the presence of thick piles of pillow lavas with an underlying system of feeder dikes that allows the lava to move up through the ocean crust.

The Prince William terrane is separated from the Yakutat terrane by several fault systems: the Chugach-Saint Elias, Ragged Mountain and Kayak Island. Farther to the west the Pacific plate is actively being subducted under the Prince William terrane along the Aleutian megathrust.

Thick hoarfrost, the result of sudden freezing and moisture-laden air, coats shrubs in the Copper River delta. Moisture is no stranger to Copper River country, where Cordova receives an average of 167 inches of precipitation annually. Temperatures, while usually milder than those farther inland, average 54 degrees F in July and 21 degrees F in January. (Ruth Fairall)

FLOWERS OF THE COPPER TRAIL

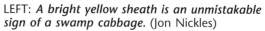

LEFT: *A bright yellow sheath is an unmistakable sign of a swamp cabbage.* (Jon Nickles)

ABOVE: *This closeup shows the delicate frills of the buckbean flower. Roots of this plant, though bitter, are edible if other, better tasting food is unavailable.* (Jon Nickles)

RIGHT: *Buckbean and horsetail characterize much of the Copper River delta's wetlands.* (Jon Nickles)

RIGHT: *Several species of columbine grow in different habitats from Alaska to the Pacific Northwest. The red columbine flourishes from southcentral Alaska south to California. Hikers can eat the flowers in moderate quantities, but should avoid consuming the other parts of the plant.* (Jon Nickles)

BELOW: *Showy wild iris add a splash of color along Alaganik Slough.* (Jon Nickles)

ABOVE: *The parasite broomrape lacks chlorophyll and draws nourishment from other plants. Authorities on wild plants claim that broomrape can be eaten, and its rootstalk boiled to make tea.* (Jon Nickles)

Yellow pond lilies bloom near Alaganik Slough in the Chugach National Forest in late June and throughout July. (Ruth Fairall)

Yakutat Terrane

The small area of the Yakutat terrane exposed along the southern Alaska coast contains Bering and Malaspina glaciers, two of the largest piedmont glaciers in North America. This terrane is also made up of some of the youngest rocks that are being added to Alaska. An older sequence of sandstones, 20 to 50 million years old, contains pieces of rocks and minerals that are not found in adjacent areas. A younger sequence, less than 20 million years old, is composed of material that was locally eroded from adjacent high mountains. One of the youngest sedimentary units, the Yakataga Formation, shows

Childs Glacier, one of the two much-visited glaciers near the end of the Copper River Highway, reaches the Copper River near the head of the delta by the Million Dollar Bridge. The glacier threatened, from time to time, to block work on the Copper River & Northwestern Railway. (Charles E. Kay)

evidence of glaciation beginning about 6 million years ago and continuing periodically to the present.

Geologic and fossil evidence suggests that the Yakutat terrane was transported to its present position from a point about 600 miles to the south during the late Cenozoic (50 to 2 million

years ago) by slippage along the Chugach-Saint Elias fault system. This trip north is thought to have begun about 25 million years ago.

Tectonics

The northern Gulf of Alaska region is a tectonically complex and active area that lies between the eastern end of the Aleutian trench and the active volcanoes of the Wrangell Mountains. In this region, the continental margin is being underthrust by the Pacific plate at an average rate of 2.5 inches per year. This zone forms a surface that dips northward at about a 10-degree angle and reaches inland to beneath the Alaska Range. The 1964 earthquake released almost 900 years of accumulated strain during

From time to time, Steller Glacier, an arm of Bering Glacier, has dammed Berg Lake, northeast of Katalla. In July 1983, this ice dam ruptured, sending water roaring into Bering and Gandil rivers and Bering Lake. U.S. Geological Survey geologists estimated that the lake's level sank 210 feet. (Marti Miller, USGS)

which time the continental and Pacific plates were locked along this section of the northern gulf coast.

Horizontal and vertical displacements related to the 1964 earthquake affected the entire region. The continental margin extending from north of Anchorage to the Gulf of Alaska was displaced seaward at least 60 feet and warped such that some areas sunk about seven feet, while other

This unusual sight occurred in January 1984 in backwater of the river flowing from Sheridan Glacier. After the river had been frozen solid for two weeks, a maritime storm brought above-freezing temperatures, rain and high winds. As a result, the ice broke up, and chunks piled up in the backwater. They subsequently froze together, forming a multi-faceted prism for the sun setting to the south. (Ruth Fairall)

A geologist inspects metasedimentary rock fragments that were incorporated in this granite intrusion north of *Wernicke Glacier.* (Marti Miller, USGS)

LEFT: *Whale Island rises at center and the Don Miller Hills in the background in this view looking northeast across Katalla Bay. The ghost town of Katalla is clustered on the bay's western shore. The hills were named for Don Miller, U.S. Geological Survey geologist who drowned in 1961 while doing field work for the survey.* (Marti Miller, USGS)

RIGHT: *Workers take a break and pose for the photographer on Katalla Co.'s No. 2 steam shovel in June 1904.* (Courtesy of Steve McCutcheon)

BOTTOM: *Katalla was a true boom town, springing up quickly during the heyday of Katalla oil field exploration and production, and dying just as quickly once oil speculation ceased. The main street, shown in this undated photo, was lined with hotels, restaurants and saloons.* (Ray Moss Collection, Alaska Historical Library)

rebuilt, as the cost outweighed the potential profit. A total of 154,000 barrels of Katalla oil were produced, but Katalla's place as the first producing oil field in Alaska is often overlooked or forgotten.

Katalla's population declined to 84 in 1920, 44 in 1930 and just 23 by 1940. The post office closed in 1943. Today, little remains of Katalla's dreams except its mineral wealth, which sporadically causes the question of building a spur road to the coal and oil fields to be raised.

Michael J. Heney:
Irish Prince

By Nicki J. Nielsen

*I*ntrepid railroad builder Michael J. Heney once remarked, "Give me enough dynamite and snoose and I'll build a road to hell!"

He got an early start when he left his home in Pembroke, Ontario, Canada at age 14 to seek his fortune working on the Canadian Pacific Railroad. The son of an Irish immigrant farmer, Heney had little interest in school. By age 21, he was a railroad contractor.

Heney first experienced Alaska working for the Anchor Point Gold Mining Company on the Kenai Peninsula. Soon afterward, he heard about the Klondike gold strike, and after months of reading about the area, arrived in Skagway in March 1898.

Almost immediately, he began plans to build a railroad through the mountains to the gold fields. He concluded that Chilkoot Pass was not feasible, but White Pass, although fraught with construction obstacles, could be conquered. After obtaining financial backing from the Close Brothers banking firm in London, Heney forged ahead. On July 6, 1899, the White Pass and Yukon Railway reached Bennett; on July 29, 1900, the rails stretched to Whitehorse. Heney had succeeded, taming the terror of the trek to the Klondike with iron rails.

A rough, hard worker who inspired loyalty in his men, Heney never asked anyone to do anything he would not do. Nervy and big-hearted, Heney gave his life for the Copper Trail: He was on the steamship *Ohio* en route to Cordova with construction materials when it sank in August 1909. He never regained his health after becoming chilled rescuing passengers and horses from the vessel, and he died of pulmonary tuberculosis 14 months later at age 45.

Rex Beach based his novel *The Iron Trail* (1912) on Heney. Beach spent several months with Heney during construction of the Copper River & Northwestern Railway. The words of Murray O'Neil (Beach's character based on Heney) when a breakwater washed away may well sum up Heney's reaction:

In a dream. . . . I saw a deserted fishing village become a thriving city. I saw the glaciers part to pass a great traffic in men and merchandise. I saw the unpeopled north grow into a land of homes, of farms, of mining camps, where people lived and bred children. I heard the mountain passes echo to steam whistles and the whir of flying wheels. It was a wonderful vision that I saw. . . . They called me a fool, and it took the sea and the hurricane to show them I was right.

PART OF CONSTRUCTION STAFF—COPPER RIVER & NORTH WESTERN RAILWAY

Left to right: ALFRED WILLIAMS, Asst. Chief Engineer; M. J. HENEY, Contractor; P. J. O'BRIEN, Bridges; E. C. HAWKINS, Chief Engineer; JAS. ENGLISH, Track Supt.; SAM MURCHISON, Supt. Construction; DR. F. B. WHITING, Chief Surgeon.

Michael J. Heney (second from left) poses with other Copper River & Northwestern Railway construction workers in this photo taken from **Grit, Grief and Gold** *(1933), Dr. F.B. Whiting's biography of Heney.* (Courtesy of Peacock Publishing Company)

Buckets of ore arrive by overhead tram at the Kennecott Copper Co.'s Bonanza Mine. In 1916 the tram was handling about 400 tons per day of copper ore.
(Norma Hoyt, courtesy of Nicki Nielsen)

prospectors. They noted, studied and described as geologically important the limestone-greenstone contact, the dominant structure along which the copper ore bodies of the Kennecott Mines occur.

In 1900, Stephen Birch, a New York mineralogist who had been employed as an Army Scout on Abercrombie's expedition the previous year, purchased several significant copper claims in the Wrangell Mountains. He sold them to the Guggenheims, who began building a railroad, first from Valdez and later from Katalla, to transport the ore to the coast.

In 1904, Michael J. Heney, at loose ends since completing his White Pass and Yukon Railway, received an enticing proposal from the London banking firm that had financed his White Pass project: If Heney could come up with a better route for a railroad through the Copper River region than the ones that had been proposed, he could count on them again for financing. After checking out ideas for routes, Heney filed for a right-of-way up the Copper River through Abercrombie Canyon to the Interior.

To assure adequate funding to complete the railroad, Heney and his London bankers approached the Alaska Syndicate with their plans. The syndicate rejected their proposal in favor of a route from Valdez through Keystone Canyon or one from Katalla, an area of interest because of nearby coal fields.

Heney was still convinced that his Copper River route from Eyak, where there was a sheltered harbor, was the best choice. He decided to begin construction on his own, and on March 13, 1906, his advance party arrived and set up a tent camp. On March 26, a brief ceremony was held to organize a new town, called Cordova. Railroad construction workers and equipment began arriving immediately, and work commenced clearing land for the railbed. On August 26 the first railroad spike was driven.

Knowing he lacked funds to complete his railroad, Heney convinced the Alaska Syndicate to purchase his Abercrombie Canyon right-of-way. As part of the arrangement, Heney agreed to retire from building the railroad. The syndicate abandoned work at Cordova and in 1907 began construction at Katalla, starting with a massive breakwater to protect the harbor from fierce storms that had occurred there since a strong earthquake in 1899.

After storms washed away the expensive breakwater shortly after its completion in fall 1907, engineer E.C. Hawkins arrived to evaluate the syndicate's options. Hawkins recommended Cordova, Heney's preferred site, as the railroad terminus. The syndicate agreed, moved their operations to Cordova and hired Heney to build their Copper River & Northwestern Railway.

As railroad work increased, the Cordova townsite became desirable for railroad expansion. On May 19, 1908, the sale of lots began at a new townsite, the location of downtown Cordova today. About $100,000 was spent on street improvements that first year, including blasting streets out of solid rock.

Cordova boomed, and the press predicted a rosy future. The December 1910 *Alaska-Yukon Magazine* claimed that Cordova's commercial growth had been unparalleled by any other Alaskan city, and that "The routing of the winter mail by way of Cordova to Fairbanks, the Iditarod, Nome and Yukon River points is the final 'O.K.' on Cordova as a gateway to Alaska."

In 1900, Eyak's population had been 222. The 1910 Cordova census was 1,152, with hundreds more employed along the railroad construction route. The main line went 130.7 miles to Chitina, where it met the Alaska road system. A 65-mile branch went to the Kennecott copper mines. Bridging the Copper River at Childs and Miles glaciers, a span later known as the "Million Dollar

Ramshackle frame buildings line the main street of Cordova's original location, known today as "Old Town." The tramway tracks, which appear to have doubled as a sidewalk, led from the water to the cannery. This postcard photo was taken in June 1908, one month after the sale of lots began on the new townsite. The postcard's message describes the scene: "This gives you a very good idea of the little town I'm in. . . . This is the main street down through Cordova. The new townsite is back a ways." (Courtesy of Nicki Nielsen)

Bridge," proved to be a dramatic construction feat. F.B. Whiting, in his 1933 biography of Heney, *Grit, Grief and Gold*, describes it:

Resting upon the solid ice below, a forest of heavy timbers gave temporary support to the network of steel above, from whose dizzy heights sturdy workmen moved about in their hazardous duties, toiling desperately to forestall the now overdue spring break-up of the river below. . . . Another hour would tell, by which time the thousands of tons of steel would become welded together and swung into permanent position as Alaska's mammoth bridge. Failure meant a twisted mass of junk, and a wholesale slaughter of men. But the glaciers on each side were now coming to life, after the long winter's lock-up, and had already begun thundering an emphatic and ominous defiance with deafening crashes of ice. . . .

. . . Anxious faces gazed intently, as dozens of wedges shot out and powerful electric jacks released their support, and a mountain

Workers pose in summer 1919 on the wood-burning engine of the Alaska Anthracite Railroad, a 22-mile line which in 1918 became the first railroad to reach the Katalla oil fields. (Myra McDonald, courtesy of Nicki Nielsen)

Early Days in Chitina

Photos courtesy of Steve McCutcheon

Editor's note: Longtime Alaskan photographer Steve McCutcheon was born in Chitina August 30, 1911. His family moved to Anchorage in 1915, but through the years he has gathered these photos, offering a glimpse of early days in one of the key communities along the Copper Trail.

This view shows the town probably in the late teens after construction of the Copper River & Northwestern Railway was completed. Chitina is located just over a small ridge from the west bank of the Copper River and 66 miles northeast of Valdez. The town was established about 1908 to supply railroad crews and miners working in the Wrangell Mountains.

Riverboats carried the bulk of summertime passengers and freight throughout much of early day Alaska, even on the turbulent Copper River. From left lie the Tonsina, Chitina and Nizina, part of the Copper River fleet, in July 1910.

Not to be outdone in cleanliness, these bear cubs partake of the Chitina Baths.

A surveyor for the Copper River & Northwestern Railway displays the one-dog power of his velocipede.

There seems to be no end to the creative transportation methods used in Chitina. Here "Long John" Carlson shows off his Chevrolet snowmobile.

*Homegrown music rings through the air
of historic Chitina.*

*H.H. "Bert" McCutcheon (shown here) and Harry
Nelson owned a saloon in Chitina in 1909. Later
McCutcheon became Road Overseer, and in 1910
married Clara J. Kreuger. The November 11, 1910,
Cordova Daily Alaskan gives this account of
McCutcheon's organization of the first sleigh ride over
the Chitina Cut-off: "...Bert McCutcheon gave the first
sleighing party of the season this week, and as the
party was the first to leave from Chitina over the new
cut-off trail, quite a few of the citizens bundled up in
real Arctic style and gathered around the sleigh to have
a picture made.by.O.W. Kennedy, official photographer
for the Katalla Co.*

*"The party consisted of Mesdames Burrows and
Newhouse, Messrs. McCutcheon, Bennett and Alba, the
latter owning the horse and sleigh. The party went as
far as the first roadhouse on Poppel Lake, a distance
between nine and ten miles...."*

Maps of European countries hang on the wall in this glimpse of early day school life at Chitina.

of steel gradually settled into permanent position with an uncanny mathematical precision, and rested. The now famous "Miles Glacier Bridge" had become a reality. . . .

Exactly one hour later, as if humanely timed, the long anticipated and much feared spring breakup became a reality. . . . A tangled mass of snapping timbers toppled and crashed into the swirling ice field below. . . . It had done its part and saved the day. . . .

In *Copper Tints* (1923) author Katherine Wilson described Cordova after the construction phase:

Other times and other manners! The day is past when the Red Dragon, as a frontier mission of the Episcopal Church, served as the amusement rendezvous for as rough and lawless a band as ever filled a beer-mug with twenty-dollar pieces for a sky-pilot [preacher]. The building of the Copper River and Northwestern Railway, bringing Cordova into existence and in its trail three thousand pick-and-shovel men, lumber-jacks, engineers, dynamiters, surveyors, clerks, adventurers, and what-not, has long since been completed. The twenty-six saloons that graced the business street have given way to ladies' specialty shops and fancy groceries. . . .

In 1911, Cordovans showed their feistiness. Earlier the federal government withdrew coal, oil and timber lands in Alaska from entry, meaning no claims could be staked and title could not be

The Copper River & Northwestern Railway's rotary plow makes its way through a cut in deep winter snows along the railroad line. (Courtesy of Nicki Nielsen)

obtained to federal lands already staked. As thousands of acres of high-grade coal in the nearby Bering River field became unavailable, Alaskans were forced to import exorbitantly priced Canadian coal from more than 1,000 miles away. Protests to the government were ignored. After years of patience, Cordova residents had reached the desperation point.

On May 3, 1911, 300 angry Cordovans armed with shovels marched to the Alaska Steamship Company dock. Chanting "Give us Alaskan coal!," they proceeded to pitch tons of Canadian coal into the bay. The president of the Chamber of Commerce led the group, which included an ex-mayor, City Council members and most of the town businessmen and professionals. As the U.S. Deputy Marshal was conveniently 3 miles away, workmen from the railway shops arrived to back up the steamship agent. Finally the Chief of Police, armed with a federal warrant, ordered the shovelers to disperse. Their leader retorted, "Shovel away, boys. We want Alaskan coal!" When ordered to disband or be arrested, the protesters shouldered their shovels and departed.

By the next morning, press wires throughout the country flashed with news of the "Cordova Coal Party." Eventually the laws were modified, and Alaskans were appeased.

Following World War I, tourism to Cordova was actively promoted. Miles and Childs glaciers, at railroad mile 48, became major attractions. Passengers could get off the train at Chitina and ride to Fairbanks in comfort in Studebaker motor stages (sight-seeing trucks), staying at well-known roadhouses along the way such as the Tonsina Lodge on the Richardson Trail. Or, they could detour to McCarthy to stay in a luxurious hotel, see the world-famous Kennecott mines and plan sheep hunting excursions in the Wrangells. Rex Beach's widely read novel, *The Iron Trail* (1912), romanticized the building of the railroad. Advertising literature made Cordova sound as if it had a corner on the market for Northland glitter as well as copper.

In 1923 President Warren G. Harding, having come to Alaska to drive the golden spike marking completion of the Alaska Railroad, visited Cordova. For Harding's visit, Cordova's children gathered on a hillside, forming a great letter "A" and singing "Alaska, My Alaska." The President rode a special train to Miles and Childs glaciers, briefly driving the train on the return trip. The celebration was ironic, as the very purpose for Harding's visit to Alaska represented an end to Cordova's role as gateway to the Interior. The

selection of Seward as ocean terminus for the Alaska Railroad dashed hopes for railroad expansion north from Chitina to the Interior.

Cordova became popularly associated with Kennecott and copper. The Kennecott mines operated from 1911 until late 1938, when they were permanently closed. Territory of Alaska records value the copper ore extracted from the mines at $287 million. Silver and other by-products were also mined.

In 1910, the majority of Cordova's 1,152 residents were railroad construction workers. The 1920 population of 1,275 included railroad employees, shopkeepers, cannery workers and fishermen. When the last train rolled into Cordova on November 11, 1938, about 300 railroad jobs ended. Many people assumed Cordova would be devastated; however, 1940 census figures show a decrease of only 43 residents from 1930.

Copper production peaked in 1916, when the Copper River & Northwestern Railway hauled nearly 100 million pounds of ore. Each day that year, the Bonanza tramway handled about 750,000 pounds of 7.5 percent mill ore and 50,000 pounds of high grade ore averaging 50 percent copper. Kennecott's famous Jumbo high grade stope, one of the richest blocks of copper ore ever mined, alone produced 140 million pounds of 70 percent copper ore during its production years. In 1916 the Jumbo tramway daily carried 800,000 pounds of 7.5 percent mill ore and 350,000 pounds of 70 percent ore. Production dropped rapidly, however, and in the 1920s averaged about 50 million pounds per year.

Copper prices fluctuated widely, from 14 cents per pound during the mines' first years, rising to 21 cents by 1919, dropping to 10 cents and then

Newspaperman Ernest Forrest Jessen expressed his opinions and took potshots at public figures in The Weekly Bull, *published in the 1920s. After 10 years as a reporter for the Cordova* Times, *Jessen went on to work in Anchorage and eventually settled in Fairbanks, where he established and published* Jessen's Weekly *(later called the* All-Alaska Weekly*) until his death in 1971.* (Courtesy of Nicki Nielsen)

continuing to rise and fall erratically throughout the 1920s. When prices dropped to 5 cents per pound in 1932, the mines did not open, and only reopened after the price was set at 9 cents in 1935. Production that year was less than 1 million pounds.

As it became obvious that the main copper ore bodies had been mined out, production interruptions and tonnage decreases helped Cordovans prepare for the time when mining and the railroad would no longer be a part of their economy. Bonuses paid to railroad employees at the end of 1938 softened the pain of the railroad's closure. More than 200 workers moved

to company operations in Utah, and others found work on the Alaska Railroad, but many stayed in Cordova and pursued other financial opportunities.

Perhaps the reason these people remained had something to do with what longtime Cordova fisherman Jack DeVille once noted when asked why he felt people stayed after the railroad closed:

> When the tide was out the table was set here. You had clams, you had crab, you had halibut, and you had salmon. You had ducks and geese. . . . This is subsistence. . . .

Fishing

As Cordova's population burgeoned during the heyday of the railroad and the Kennecott mines, fishing also boomed and became an important part of the town's economy.

In 1915, the Cordova commercial razor clam fishery began, producing an average of nearly 1 million pounds annually and dominating the industry for many years. A crab industry also developed, and between 1935 and 1940 an average of more than half a million crab were canned each year at seven Cordova-area plants. The herring catch also increased in the 1930s, growing from a 7,664-ton pack in 1931 to 52,859 tons by 1939.

But the most important fishery then, as now, was salmon. Through the years, the salmon fishery changed as new regulations limited areas, gear and fishing periods. The industry grew significantly during the 1920s, but there were few independent fishermen because most boats were company-owned. Highly effective fish traps and

Haven for 1930s Cordovans was Nirvana Park, brainchild
of early Cordova businessman Henry C. Feldman. The park
included trails, statues, fountains and natural sculptures
made from burls. Borders were planted in wildflowers
which Feldman had collected. (Courtesy of Nicki Nielsen)

Eustace P. Ziegler: Missionary Artist

By Nicki J. Nielsen

Eustace Ziegler works on a landscape in this 1924 photo. Ziegler came to Cordova as a lay Episcopal missionary in 1909 and stayed until the mid-1920s. (The Episcopal Diocese of Alaska, from *The Alaskan Churchman*; reprinted from *The ALASKA JOURNAL®*)

*I*n January 1909, a short, slender clergyman's son descended the steamship gangplank at boomtown Cordova. Boyhood years spent around the Detroit docks and doing odd jobs around logging camps prepared him for the rough atmosphere of this raw frontier town.

A lay missionary at the Red Dragon Clubhouse (part of Cordova's Episcopal mission) and later a priest and designer of Cordova's St. George's Episcopal Church, Ziegler traveled the Copper River & Northwestern line and made visits along the coast. These trips provided much material for the budding artistic career nurtured during his Cordova years, a career which earned him a reputation as one of Alaska's foremost pioneer artists.

Ziegler's paintings portrayed Natives, prospectors, workers and adventurers and their relationships to Alaska. In contrast to Sydney Laurence (with whom his work is often compared), Ziegler's landscapes teem with human activity. While at the Red Dragon he edited *The Alaskan Churchman*, gracing its pages with woodcuts, sketches and articles which display considerable writing skill. His first recorded one-man art show was held 1,200 feet underground in the Kennecott mines dining room, the only place large enough for the show.

Ziegler's days in Cordova were apparently happy ones. In a May 11, 1958, letter to the Rev. Lewis Hodgkins at St. George's Church, Ziegler recalled his time there:

I arrived in Cordova in Jan. 1909, so my 50th anniversary is also upon me soon. I wish I were as rich and prosperous now as I was at that time, getting $750 a year and living in the Red Dragon — a tent beside it. The Red Dragon and Cordova paid me more than I can express.

E.T. Stannard, president of Alaska Steamship Company, purchased a Ziegler mountain scene about 1911. In

1924, Stannard offered Ziegler a commission to paint a series of murals for the company's Seattle offices. Ziegler accepted and moved to Seattle, returning summers to Alaska to sketch and paint, often near Mount McKinley. In Seattle, Ziegler supported his family entirely through his art, garnering this headline in the May 4, 1947, *Seattle Times*: "Ziegler, An Artist Who Eats Regularly."

Ziegler painted until shortly before he died in 1969 at age 87. Through his art, he left a visual treasure capturing the Alaska he experienced in the early 20th century.

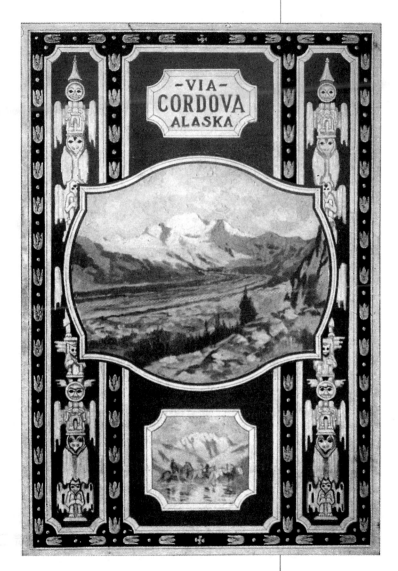

Eustace Ziegler was a prolific artist and illustrator during the years he spent in Alaska. Examples of his artwork adorn the covers of Via Cordova Alaska, *a promotional brochure produced by the Cordova Chamber of Commerce, probably in the mid-1920s, and* The Alaskan Churchman, *Episcopal Church publication which Ziegler edited for a time in Cordova. For the* Churchman *cover, Ziegler adapted his nativity scene to Alaska, depicting the three wise men as a fisherman, a miner and a trapper. (Top, The Episcopal Diocese of Alaska, courtesy of Nicki Nielsen; right,* ALASKA GEOGRAPHIC® *files)*

"Horse Creek Mary," was one of Ziegler's favorite subjects; this drawing appeared in the Churchman *in October 1923.* (The Episcopal Diocese of Alaska, reprinted from *The Alaska Journal*®)

For many years, the U.S. Navy operated a radio station (shown here in 1927) at Mile Seven on the Copper River & Northwestern Railway. (Courtesy of Nicki Nielsen)

purse seines were the mainstay in Prince William Sound. (The traps, though widely used, caused a severe depletion of the fishing resource and were outlawed in 1959 with statehood.) In the 1930s fishermen and cannery workers organized strikes which resulted in higher fish prices and the emergence of strong fisheries unions.

Jack DeVille described the years 1934 and 1935, when fishermen and cannery workers struck for decent wages. During the strike, U.S. Secretary of Labor Frances Perkins sent federal mediator Charles Johnson Post to talks between the strikers and the cannery owners. DeVille, a member of the fishermen's negotiating committee, remembers Mr. Post stating at the end of the talks:

"Now here we have all the packers here in one room with the negotiating committee so I want to tell you one thing.

"You men have been robbing [the fishermen] blind. They're finally getting a decent wage. The only trouble is what they ask for this year, their getting price that you'll give them is going to be one year behind. . . ."

In 1938 more than half the approximately 1,000 fishermen employed in the Prince William Sound region were Cordova residents. Area canneries employed about 1,500 persons, more than a third of whom were from Cordova or nearby native villages. By 1938, Cordovans directly employed in the fishing industry totaled about five times the number of railroad employees.

The 1964 earthquake brought about dramatic changes in the Cordova fisheries. In addition to destroying clam beds, salmon spawning streams were changed radically, and the general uplift of the delta caused a major reduction in the fishing area. Despite these changes, however, the Cordova fishery remains rich, and today the industry forms the community's economic base.

The U.S. Coast Guard has had a place on the Cordova waterfront since 1935, when the cutter *Haida* was first stationed there. In 1938 the *Spencer* replaced the *Haida*, followed later by other cutters including, most recently, the *Sorrel* and the *Sweetbriar*. The *Sweetbriar* continues to patrol Cordova area waters, repairing navigational aids, conducting search and rescue operations and

Two or three times each week during the summer, the Alaska state ferry **Bartlett** *makes the run between Cordova, Valdez and Whittier.* (Rose Arvidson)

Wildlife of the Copper Trail

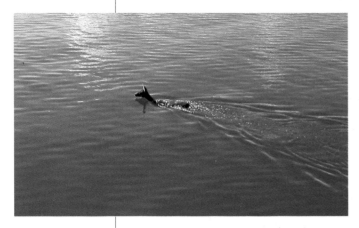

ABOVE: *A Sitka black-tailed deer swims from the mainland to Hawkins Island, where two dozen of the animals were introduced in the 1920s. Because they are superb swimmers and well-adapted to the habitat, the deer rapidly spread throughout the islands of Prince William Sound and to the mainland. Today, they are the most commonly taken big game in the area.* (Ruth

ABOVE: *Dall sheep, the only white, wild sheep in the world, inhabit mountainous areas along the Copper Trail. The animals eat a variety of grasses and other vegetation, and in winter can dig down through the snow to reach food. Dall sheep breed from late November through mid-December; lambs, which weigh 5 to 6 pounds, are born from mid-May through mid-June.* (George Wuerthner)

LEFT: *A white-tailed ptarmigan, one of three ptarmigan species in the state and the one with the greatest preference for high country, suns itself on this rocky perch in the Wrangell Mountains.* (Chlaus Lotscher)

North America's largest waterfowl, regal trumpeter swans nest on the Copper River delta where the big white bodies, sitting on nesting mounds, are visible from the Copper River Highway.
(Kent Wranic)

A black bear feeds on sedges in a coastal area. The bears are omnivorous, eating a wide range of food, from salmon to clover to tree bark. The animals reach weights of 100 to 200 pounds (occasionally more), and can be seen in various color phases, including brown, blue-gray or cinnamon.
(George Wuerthner)

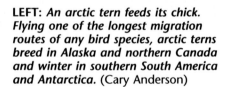

RIGHT: *Rocky shorelines covered with barnacles, mussels and kelp in the Mummy Island area make fine habitat for these wandering tattlers.* (Rose Arvidson)

BELOW: *A sea otter feeds on crab, which, with other shellfish, makes up an important part of the animals' diet. Sea otters are common in Orca Inlet, a prime wintering ground for males of the species. After being hunted to near extinction for their prized pelts, sea otters were given complete protection from hunting in 1911. Their populations have increased through the years, and today Prince William Sound is home to a healthy number of otters.* (Ruth Fairall)

LEFT: *An arctic tern feeds its chick. Flying one of the longest migration routes of any bird species, arctic terns breed in Alaska and northern Canada and winter in southern South America and Antarctica.* (Cary Anderson)

BOTTOM: *This photo shows some of the more than 40 species of shorebirds that have been observed on the Copper River delta: ruddy turnstones (heavy black markings on face and breast); black turnstone (large bird in center); short-billed dowitcher (two birds with bills tucked under wing at lower left); dunlin (black bellies); western sandpiper (the smaller birds interspersed throughout the flock). The entire western population of dunlins use the delta during spring migration.* (Ruth Fairall)

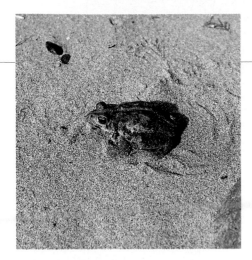

Dusky Canada geese breed only on the Copper River delta and on Middleton Island. The 1964 earthquake severely reduced quality breeding habitat for this species when uplift of the land gave predators much greater access to nesling areas. Populations of duskies have declined since, despite efforts of biologists to hinder predator movement and establish breeding populations elsewhere. (Rose Arvidson)

ABOVE: *Amphibians are often missing from lists of Alaskan wildlife, yet two species of frogs, one toad and three salamanders can be found in various parts of the state. The northern limit of the amphibians' range depends on the length of summer — the animals must have about 100 days without a killing frost to complete their cycle of reproduction and metamorphosis before winter sets in. Northern amphibians hibernate in shallow depressions they dig in the ground, relying on dead vegetation and snowfall for insulation. Often seen in coastal areas, this boreal toad was spotted on the beach at Point Martin, located at the northwest end of Controller Bay, about three miles southwest of Katalla.* (Marti Miller, USGS)

RIGHT: *A moose takes a dip in Two-Mile Lake, near Chitina, looking for water plants. Largest living member of the deer family, Alaskan moose weigh in at 1,000 to 1,600 pounds for males; 800 to 1,200 pounds for cows. Moose are a prime target of subsistence and sport hunters.* (Harry Walker)

Fishing the Copper River and Prince William Sound

By Dan Strickland

Editor's note: *Dan Strickland is a fisherman and writer who makes his home in Cordova.*

Just to the east of Prince William Sound tendrils of the powerful Copper River spill out over a vast delta and enter the Pacific Ocean. The Copper River and the Sound are sisters geographically, but if they are of the same family, they were spawned by wildly different gods. From Point Whitshed, south of Cordova, westward lie

The 1964 earthquake uplifted land near the mouth of the Copper River as much as six feet, thus rendering inaccessible an area that formerly offered lucrative fishing to seiners. This seiner works much deeper waters in Prince William Sound. (Rose Arvidson)

the deep fiords and relatively calm waters of the Sound. To the east stretch a treacherous hundred miles of shallow bars and hammering surf. Savage winds can sweep down across the Sound and roil her waters, but the song of the Copper River delta is one of storms and wind and thundering waves, and echoes of angry surf linger even as the Gulf falls quiet, much as a seashell holds the ocean's cadence.

Before the great earthquake of 1964, the water on the delta was deeper. Seine boats as well as gillnetters were able to fish for returning salmon in front of the river mouth itself. But in the cataclysmic upheaval of Good Friday 1964 the land was thrust six feet higher, and accessibility to the rich fishing grounds was almost lost to the fleet. Seining the Copper River was now but a memory of experienced fishermen.

Although not caught commercially, rockfish are a frequent take of sport fishermen in eastern Prince William Sound, and the Department of Fish and Game has recently instituted bag limits for these fish. The most important rockfish of the area include: yelloweye (shown in photos), silvergray, copper and quillback. (Ruth Fairall)

Only drift gillnetting remained.

After the quake a series of low sandbars faced the Gulf of Alaska. Behind this thin veneer of protection are the sloughs and shallows which make up the "Flats," as the delta is known locally. These waters join behind the bars, and empty into the Gulf through one of several channels: Strawberry, Egg Island, Pete Dahl, Grass Island, Kokenhenik and Softuk. Farther east lie the Martin Islands, Bering River and Controller Bay. Kayak Island, the site where Bering and Steller made the first landing in 1741, marks the

eastern extent of the fishing grounds.

Skiffs can travel all the way from Whitshed to Softuk behind the bars, but the tide must be high, and the capricious channels known. One passage, called the Racetrack, cuts sinuously through a wide shallow mudflat. It is usually marked by buoys or alder branches stuck in the mud, and as often as not a hapless bow-picker as well. In what may at first seem a perplexing contrast of reason, it is sometimes necessary to wait for the tide to drop to navigate the shallowest area. Several boats will often anchor at the Racetrack's mouth, waiting for the ebbing tide to reveal its banks. What looks to be an expansive ocean or lake suddenly metamorphoses into a far-reaching flatland with a swift river winding through it. Anchors are weighed, and the boats roar through single file — it's barely 20 feet from bank to bank — before the tide drops farther. There is a generous three feet of water on either side of the Racetrack, more than enough by Copper River standards.

As the topography and fishing have changed during the years, so have the vessels. Initially 20- to 30-foot wooden skiffs were fished, with a small cabin in the bow to escape the weather. Outboards provided the power, and nets were pulled by hand or by motor-driven "Lankard" reels. Much of the best fishing was, and is, found out in front of the protective bars, in the breakers rolling in from the Gulf. Since it is better to face breaking waves bow-first than to present the stern, the bow-picker has gradually become archetypical of the Copper River fishery.

Bow-pickers range from 16 to 30 feet and longer, but their cabins are aft and powerful hydraulics pull the nets over the bow. Inboard engines with outdrives, which can be raised in

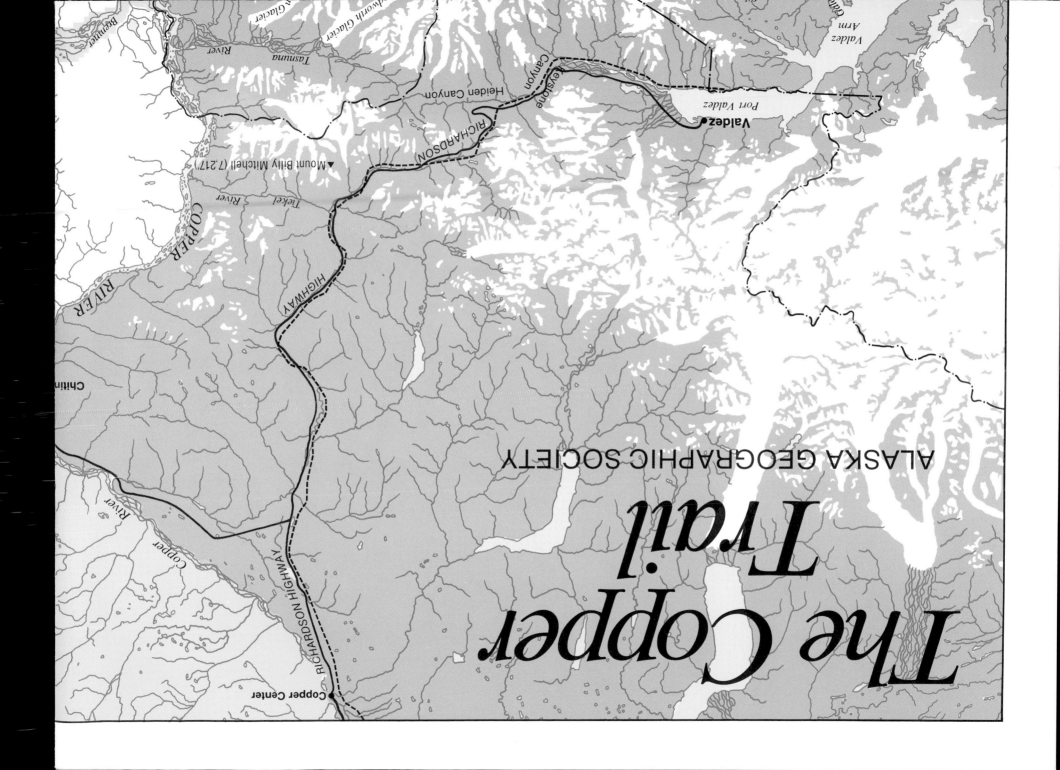

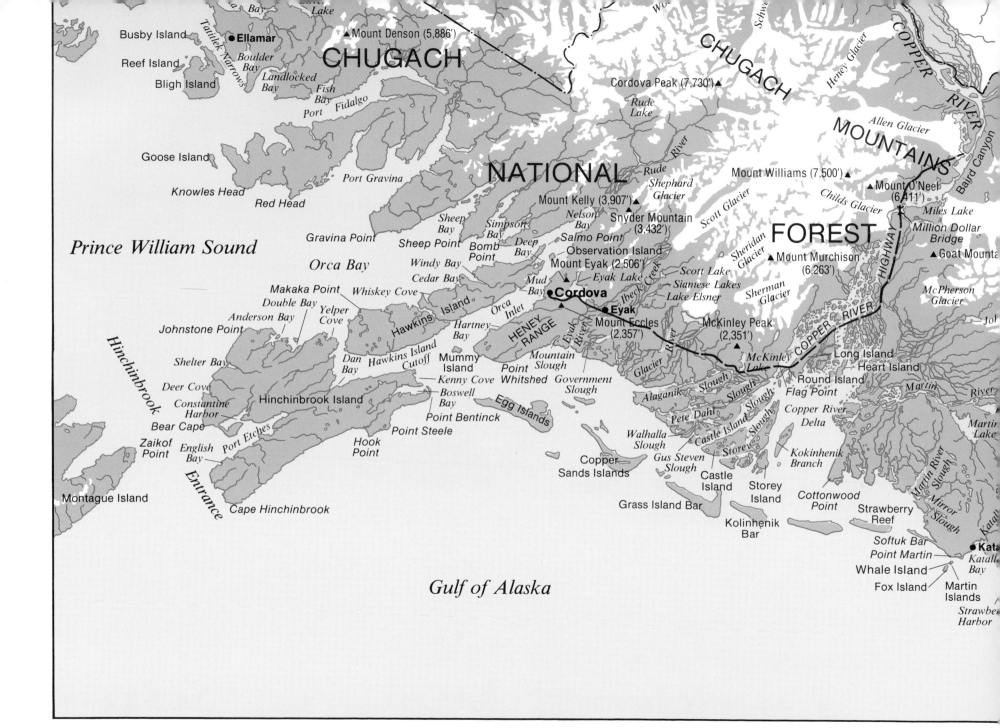

shallow water, and even jet boats which require only inches of water, have largely replaced outboards. In the last few years more skippers have been finding the fishing good in offshore waters, and stern-pickers still comprise a significant part of the fleet, though now they are of deeper draft and sturdier build than the old cabin skiffs.

The exposure to Gulf storms and the nature of the Copper River fishery make it one of Alaska's most dangerous. Each year fishermen are lost to the frigid waters. When the storms roll in — and they do with a deadly swiftness — the bars can close off or become impassable. Skippers inside the bars throw their anchors and ride out the weather as best they can, often fighting a stiff chop even in the sloughs. Those caught outside must head offshore to deeper water and wait it out, or run west to Hinchinbrook Entrance, and the safer waters of Prince William Sound.

Though it is dangerous, it is also lucrative. The fleet of 400 to 500 boats catch some 750,000 to 1,000,000 red salmon yearly. About 25,000 to 35,000 king salmon are taken early in the spring in incidental catch, and roughly 350,000 silver salmon are harvested in the fall. The revenue generated is substantial, roughly $20 million annually, but more than providing a financial

TOP: *The* **Lucky Star** *heads out of the Cordova boat harbor, while gulls reel overhead. Froth on the water is from the outtake pipe of a nearby cannery.* (Ruth Fairall)

RIGHT: *When salmon are running, fish wheels line the east bank of the Copper River near Chitina. Sockeye, or red, salmon is the species most frequently taken in this personal-use subsistence fishery.* (Chlaus Lotscher)

Stately wooden structures mark the Cordova skyline as Mount Eyak (2,506 feet) towers behind the town.
(Cary Anderson)

Displayed in a shop window is an authentic iceworm, safely encased in a block of glacier ice. Residents and visitors with competitive blood can join the survival suit races in the small boat harbor, the chili-making contest, the beard-growing competition or any one of a number of contests and events designed to ward off the effects of cabin fever.

Isolation has drawn the residents of Cordova together. Indeed, plans to breach this isolation with completion of the Copper River Highway through the mountains and up the river valley to join with the Richardson Highway coming north from Valdez stir the blood of Cordovans as much as any other issue. Some favor the proposal, some oppose it. But no matter the outcome, there is no doubt that the town born and nourished by the Copper Trail will survive. And perhaps, if the road is punched through, sounds of modern trucks and cars will echo across valleys and up hillsides that have heard little from man since that day in fall 1938, when the last train rode the rails of the Copper Trail.

Bibliography

Abercrombie, William R. *Copper River Exploring Expedition, Alaska, 1899.* Washington, D.C.: U.S. Government Printing Office, 1900.

Alaska Copper River Route. Copper River & Northwestern Railway advertising brochure, no date (ca. 1911-1912).

Alaska Geographic Society. *Alaska Steam: A Pictorial History of the Alaska Steamship Company.* Alaska Geographic® Vol. 11, No. 4, 1984.

—. *Wrangell-Saint Elias: International Mountain Wilderness.* Alaska Geographic® Vol. 8, No. 1, 1981.

Alaska-Yukon Magazine, Cordova-Chitina Number, December 1910.

Allen, Henry T. *Report of an Expedition to the Copper, Tanana, and Koyukuk Rivers in the Territory of Alaska in the Year 1885.* Washington, D.C.: U.S. Government Printing Office, 1887.

Andrews, C.L. "Making Cordova the Hub of Alaska." *Alaska-Yukon Magazine,* December 1910.

Arvidson, Rose C., et al. *Cordova, The First 75 Years.* Cordova: Fathom Publishing Company, 1984.

Beach, Rex. *The Iron Trail.* New York: Harper & Brothers, 1912.

Birket-Smith, Kaj and DeLaguna, Frederica. *The Eyak Indians of the Copper River Delta, Alaska.* Copenhagen, Denmark: Levin & Munksgaard, 1938.

Brooks, Alfred H. "Alaska Coal and its Utilization." U.S. Geological Survey Bulletin 442. Washington, D.C.: U.S. Government Printing Office, 1910.

—. "Railway Routes." U.S. Geological Survey Bulletin No. 284. Washington, D.C.: U.S. Government Printing Office, 1906.

—. "The Alaska Mining Industry in 1914." U.S. Geological Survey Bulletin 622. Washington, D.C.: U.S. Government Printing Office, 1915.

Brown, Charles M. *The Controller Bay Region: an historic resources study.* Anchorage: Alaska Division of Parks, Office of History and Archaeology, 1975.

Carlson, Phyllis D. "Alaska's Hall of Fame Painter: A Sourdough Painter Preacher." *Alaskana,* Vol. 1, No. 10, November 1971.

Charles, Sidney D. "Cordova, the New Gateway Metropolis." *Alaska-Yukon Magazine,* December 1910.

"Cordova Gateway to Interior Alaska." Cordova: Daily Alaska Print, no date (ca. 1919).

Daniel, Jan. *The Birth of a Ghost Town.* Unpublished paper, April 1979.

Douglas, William C. *A History of the Kennecott Mines, Kennecott, Alaska.* Kennecott Corporation, 1974 (reprint).

Dumoulin, J.A. "Sandstone composition of the Valdez and Orca Groups, Prince William Sound, Alaska." U.S Geological Survey Bulletin 1774, 1987.

Episcopal Church of Alaska. *The Alaskan Churchman,* May 1909.

Eustace Ziegler, A Retrospective Exhibition. Anchorage: Anchorage Historical and Fine Arts Museum, 1977.

Eyles, N. and Lagoe, M.B. "Sedimentology of shell-rich deposits (coquinas) in the glaciomarine upper Cenozoic Yakataga Formation, Middleton Island, Alaska." Geological Society of America Bulletin, vol. 101, pp. 129-142, 1989.

Grant, U.S. and Higgins, D.F. "Reconnaissance of the geology and mineral resources of Prince William Sound, Alaska." U.S. Geological Survey Bulletin 443. Washington, D.C.: U.S. Government Printing Office, 1910.

Gruening, Ernest. *The State of Alaska.* New York: Random House, 1954.

Hanable, William S. *Summary History — the Lower Copper and Chitina Rivers.* Anchorage: Alaska Division of Parks, 1972.

Haycox, Stephen W. "The Impact of the Closing of the Copper River and Northwestern Railway on Cordova, Alaska: 1938, Part I: A Statistical View." Paper presented at the Pacific Northwest History Conference, Anchorage, June 26, 1982.

Janson, Lone E. *The Copper Spike.* Anchorage: Alaska Northwest Publishing Company, 1975.

Jansons, U. and others. "Mineral Occurrences in the Chugach National Forest, southcentral Alaska." U.S. Bureau of Mines Open-file Report MLA 5-84, 1984.

Jones, D.L., Silberling, N.J., Coney, P.J. and Plafker, G. "Lithnotectonic terrane map of Alaska." U.S. Geological Survey Map MF-1874-A, 1987.

Martin, George C. "Geology and Mineral Resources of the Controller Bay Region, Alaska. Washington, D.C.: U.S. Government Printing Office, 1908.

—. "Petroleum at Controller Bay." U.S. Geological Survey Bulletin 314. Washington, D.C.: U.S. Government Printing Office, 1907.

Moffit, Fred H. and Maddren, A.G. "Mineral resources of the Kotsina-Chitina Region, Alaska. U.S. Geological Survey Bulletin 374. Washington, D.C.: U.S. Government Printing Office, 1909.

Nelson, S.W. and others. "Mineral resource potential of the Chugach National Forest, Alaska." U.S. Geological Survey Map MF 1645-A, 1984.

Nichols, D.R. "Origin of the course of the Copper River." Geological Society of America, Special Paper 73, 1963.

Nichols, Jeanette Paddock. *Alaska.* New York: Russell & Russell, 1963.

Nielsen, Nicki J. *From Fish and Copper — Cordova's Heritage and Buildings.* Alaska Historical Commission Studies in History No. 124. Cordova: Cordova Historical Society, 1984.

—. "The Impact of the Closing of the Copper River and Northwestern Railway on Cordova, Alaska: 1938, Part II: Recollections of Longtime Cordovans." Paper presented at the Pacific Northwest History Conference, Anchorage, June 26, 1982.

—. *The Red Dragon and St. George's: Glimpses Into Cordova's Past.* Cordova: Fathom Publishing Company, 1983.

Orth, Donald J. *Dictionary of Alaska Place Names.* U.S. Geological Survey Professional Paper 567. Washington, D.C.: U.S. Government Printing Office, 1967.

Payne, Jim. "Brief History of Fishing in Cordova." Cordova Iceworm Festival Booklet, 1987.

Plafker, George, et al. "Effects of the Earthquake of March 27, 1964 on Various Communities." U.S. Geological Survey Professional Paper 542-G. Washington, D.C.: U.S. Government Printing Office, 1969.

Plafker, G. "Geology of the Chugach Mountains and southern Copper River Basin, southern Alaska." In *Alaskan Geological and Geophysical Transect: American Geophysical Union Field Trip Guidebook T104,* eds. W.J. Nokleberg and M.A. Fisher, 1989.

—. "Regional geology and petroleum potential of the northern Gulf of Alaska continental margin." Circum-pacific Council for Energy and Mineral Resources, Earth Sciences series, vol. 6, pp. 229-268.

"Tectonic deformation associated with the 1964 Alaska earthquake." *Science* vol. 148: pp. 1675-1687.

Ray, Joan Alita. "Alaska's First Oil Refinery — 1911." *The Alaskana,* Vol. 1, No. 3, April 1971.

Ricks, Melvin B. *Directory of Alaska Postmasters and Post Offices.* Ketchikan: Tongass Publishing Company, 1965.

Skud, Bernard E., et al. *Statistics of the Alaska Herring Fishery, 1878-1956.* U.S. Fish and Wildlife Statistical Digest No. 48. Washington, D.C.: U.S. Fish and Wildlife Service, 1960.

Sullivan, Michael Sean. *Kennecott, Alaska: A Historic Preservation Plan.* Alaska Historical Society, 1981.

Tower, Elizabeth A. *Big Mike Heney: Irish Prince of the Iron Trails.* Anchorage: Elizabeth A. Tower, 1988.

U.S. Bureau of Commercial Fisheries. *Annual Management Report.* Washington, D.C.: U.S. Bureau of Fisheries, various years.

U.S. Fish and Wildlife Service. *Alaska Fishery and Fur Seal Industries.* Washington, D.C.: U.S. Fish and Wildlife Service, various years.

Whiting, F.B. *Grit, Grief and Gold.* Seattle: Peacock Publishing Company, 1933.

Wilson, Katherine. *Copper-Tints: A Book of Cordova Sketches.* Seattle: Shorey Bookstore (facsimile reproduction), 1966.

—. "President is Acclaimed in Cordova." *The Alaskan Churchman,* Vol. 17, No. 2, 1922.

Index

Photographers

Alaska Geographic® Back Issues

Admiralty...Island in Contention, Vol. 1, No. 3. In-depth review of Southeast's Admiralty Island. 78 pages, $7.50.

Richard Harrington's Antarctic, Vol. 3, No. 3. Reviews Antarctica and islands of southern polar regions, territories of mystery and controversy. Fold-out map. 104 pages, $12.95.

Southeast: Alaska's Panhandle, Vol. 5, No. 2. Explores southeastern Alaska's maze of fjords and islands, forests and mountains, from Dixon Entrance to Icy Bay, including all of the Inside Passsage. The book profiles every town, and reviews the region's history, economy, people, attractions and future. fold-out map. 192 pages, $15.95.

Alaska Whales and Whaling, Vol. 5, No. 4. The wonders of whales in Alaska—their life cycles, travels and travails—are examined, with an authoritative history of commercial and subsistence whaling in the North. Includes a fold-out poster of 14 major whale species in Alaska in perspective, color photos and illustrations, with historical photos and line drawings. 144 pages, $19.95.

Alaska's Native People, Vol. 6, No. 3. Examines the worlds of the Inupiat and Yupik Eskimo, Athabascan, Aleut, Tlingit, Haida and Tsimshian. Fold-out map of Native villages and language areas. 304 pages, $24.95.

The Stikine River, Vol. 6, No. 4. River route to three Canadian gold strikes, the Stikine is the largest and most navigable of several rivers that flow from northwestern Canada through southeastern Alaska to the Pacific Ocean. Fold-out map. 96 pages. $12.95.

A Photographic Geography of Alaska, Vol. 7, No. 2. A visual tour through the six regions of Alaska: Southeast, Southcentral/Gulf Coast, Alaska Peninsula and Aleutians, Bering Sea Coast, Arctic and Interior. 192 pages, $17.95.

Wrangell-Saint Elias, Vol. 8, No. 1. Alaska's only designated World Heritage Area, this mountain wilderness takes in the nation's largest national park in its sweep from the Copper River across the Wrangell Mountains to the southern tip of the Saint Elias Range near Yakutat. Fold-out map. 144 pages, $19.95.

Alaska Mammals, Vol. 8, No. 2. Reviews in anecdotes and facts the entire spectrum of Alaska's wildlife. 184 pages, $15.95.

The Kotzebue Basin, Vol. 8, No. 3. Examines northwestern Alaska's thriving trading area of Kotzebue Sound and the Kobuk and Noatak river basins. 184 pages, $15.95.

Alaska National Interest Lands, Vol. 8, No. 4. Reviews each of Alaska's national interest land (d-2 lands) selections, outlining location, size, access and briefly describes special attractions. 242 pages, $17.95.

Alaska's Glaciers, Vol. 9, No. 1. Examines in-depth the massive rivers of ice, their composition, exploration, present-day distribution and scientific significance. Illustrated with many comtemporary color and historical black-and-white photos, the text includes separate discussions of more than a dozen glacial regions. 144 pages, $19.95.

Islands of the Seals; The Pribilofs, Vol. 9, No. 3. Great herds of northern fur seals and immense flocks of seabirds share their island homeland with Aleuts brought to this remote Bering Sea outpost by Russians. 128 pages, $12.95.

Alaska's Oil/Gas & Minerals Industry, Vol. 9, No. 4. Experts detail the geological processes and resulting mineral and fossil fuel resources that contribute substantially to Alaska's economy. 216 pages, $15.95.

Adventure Roads North: The Story of the Alaska Highway and Other Roads in *The MILEPOST®.* **Vol. 10, No.1.** Reviews the history of Alaska's roads and takes a mile-by-mile look at the country they cross. 224 pages, $17.95.

Anchorage and the Cook Inlet Basin, Vol. 10, No. 2. Reviews in-depth the commercial and urban center of the Last Frontier. Three fold-out maps. 168 pages, $17.95.

Alaska's Salmon Fisheries, Vol. 10, No. 3. A comprehensive look at Alaska's most valuable commercial fishery. 128 pages. $15.95.

Up the Koyukuk, Vol. 10, No. 4. Highlights the wildlife and traditional native lifestyle of this remote region of northcentral Alaska. 152 pages, $17.95.

Nome: City of the Golden Beaches, Vol. 11, No. 1. Reviews the colorful history of one of Alaska's most famous gold rush towns. 184 pages, $14.95.

Alaska's Farms and Gardens, Vol. 11, No. 2. An overview of the past, present and future of agriculture in Alaska, with details on growing your own vegetables in the North. 144 pages, $15.95.

Chilkat River Valley, Vol. 11, No. 3. Explores the mountain-rimmed valley at the head of the Inside Passage, its natural resources, and the residents who have settled there. 112 pages, $15.95.

Alaska Steam, Vol. 11, No. 4. Pictorial history of the pioneering Alaska Steamship Company. 160 pages. $14.95.

Northwest Territories, Vol. 12, No. 1. In-depth look at the magnificent wilderness of Canada's high Arctic. Fold-out map. 136 pages, $17.95.

Alaska's Forest Resources, Vol. 12, No. 2. Examines the botanical, recreational and economic value of Alaska's forests. 200 pages, $16.95.

Alaska Native Arts and Crafts, Vol. 12, No. 3. In-depth review of the art and artifacts of Alaska's Natives. 215 pages, $17.95.

Our Arctic Year, Vol. 12, No. 4. Compelling story of a year in the wilds of the Brooks Range. 150 pages, $15.95.

Where Mountains Meet the Sea: Alaska's Gulf Coast, Vol. 13, No. 1. Alaskan's first-hand descriptions of the 850-mile arc that crowns the Pacific Ocean from Kodiak to Cape Spencer at the entrance to southeastern Alaska's Inside Passage. 191 pages, $17.95.

Backcountry Alaska, Vol. 13, No. 2. A full-color look at the remote communities of Alaska. 224 pages, $17.95.

British Columbia's Coast/The Canadian Inside Passage, Vol. 13, No. 3. Reviews the B.C. coast west of the Coast Mountain divide from mighty Vancouver and elegant Victoria in the south, to the forested wilderness to the north, including the Queen Charlotte islands. Fold-out map. 200 pages, $17.95.

Dogs of the North, Vol. 14, No. 1. The first men to cross the Bering Land Bridge probably brought dogs to Alaska. This issue examines the development of northern breeds from the powerful husky and malemute to the fearless little Tahltan bear dog, the evolution of the dogsled, uses of dogs, and the history of sled-dog racing from the All-Alaska Sweepstakes of 1908 to the nationally televised Iditarod of today. 120 pages, $16.95.

Alaska's Seward Peninsula, Vol. 14, No. 3. The Seward Peninsula is today's remnant of the Bering Land Bridge, gateway to an ancient America. This issue chronicles the blending of traditional Eskimo culture with the white man's persistent search for gold. Fold-out map. 112 pages, $15.95.

The Upper Yukon Basin, Vol. 14, No. 4. Yukoner Monty Alford describes this remote region, headwaters for one of the continent's mightiest rivers and gateway for some of Alaska's earliest pioneers. 117 pages, $17.95.

Glacier Bay: Icy Wilderness, Vol. 15, No. 1. Covers the 5,000-square-mile wilderness now known as Glacier Bay National Park and Preserve, including the natural and human history of the Glacier Bay area, its wildlife, how to get there, what to expect, and what changes now seem predictable. 103 pages, $17.95.

Dawson City, Vol. 15, No. 2. For two years just before the turn of the century, writes author Mike Doogan, news from Dawson City blazed like a nova around the world and a million people wanted to go there. Like a nova, the gold rush burned out quickly, but its light still illuminates the city it built. In this issue Doogan examines the geology and the history of the Klondike, and why a million tourists want to go to Dawson while other gold-rush towns of the North are only collapsed cabins and faded memories. 94 pages, historic and contemporary photos, index, $15.95.

Denali, Vol. 15, No. 3. It was *Denali* to the Tanana Indians, *Doleika*, to the nearby Tanainas, *Bolshaya Gora* to the Russians, all connoting size and height and scenic grandeur. A gold-prospector called it *McKinley* less than a century ago, and unfortunately that name endured. But the mountain massif in southcentral Alaska, by whatever name, has fascinated man from the primitive to the present. This book is an in-depth guide to the Great One, its lofty neighbors and the surrounding wilderness now known as Denali National Park and Preserve. 94 pages, historic and contemporary photos, index, $16.95.

The Kuskokwim River, Vol. 15, No. 4. A review of one of Alaska's most important rivers, this issue focuses on the entire Kuskokwim drainage, from the headwaters to the mouth on Kuskokwim Bay. Author Mary Lenz discusses natural and human history along the river, including mining, fishing, riverboats and village life. 94 pages, historic and contemporary photos, index, $17.95.

Katmai Country, Vol. 16, No. 1. This issue reviews the volcanic world of Katmai National Park and Preserve and adjoining Becharof National Wildlife Refuge. Home to some of the state's highest brown bear populations, this wilderness at the head of the Alaska Peninsula claims the Valley of 10,000 Smokes and its famous volcanoes. The natural and cultural history of one of Alaska's most turbulent landscapes comes to life in *Katmai Country*. 96 pages, $17.95.

North Slope Now, Vol. 16, No. 2. Much has changed on Alaska's northern fringe since our original issue was prepared on the North Slope: the trans-Alaska pipeline, vastly expanded oil development, major new mineral finds, the debate over the Arctic National Wildlife Refuge. This issue will remind readers of the isolated world north of the Brooks Range and bring them up-to-date on the economic forces that have propelled the slope into the limelight. 96 pages, $14.95.

The Tanana Basin, Vol. 16, No. 3. For more than a century rivers were the door for opening Alaska's great Interior. One of the major corridors was the Tanana, tributary to the Yukon. Although the basin held out against the influx of westerners until this century, it has now become the urban heart of interior Alaska. This issue acquaints readers with the contempory lifestyle of Alaska's heartland and recounts her glorious and exciting history. 96 pages, $17.95.

NEXT ISSUE:

The Nushagak River, Vol. 17, No. 1. Few rivers of western Alaska carry the historical and commercial impact of the Nushagak, a short, but mighty, stream in Bristol Bay country. This issue reviews this important corridor for ancient men and early Westerners, and details the lifestyle and resources of one of the world's largest commercial fisheries. With fold-out map. To members early 1990. Price to be announced.

ALL PRICES SUBJECT TO CHANGE.

Your $39 membership in The Alaska Geographic Society includes four subsequent issues of *ALASKA GEOGRAPHIC®*, the Society's official quarterly. Please add $4 for non-U.S. membership.

Additional membership information is available upon request. Single copies of the *ALASKA GEOGRAPHIC®* back issues are also available. When ordering, please make payments in U.S. funds. All prices include postage. To order back issues, send your check or money order and volumes desired to:

The Alaska Geographic Society

P.O. Box 93370, Anchorage, Alaska 99509